WORTH KNOWING

Megan Hartford

Manhattan, Kansas
2023

PRAISE FOR WORTH KNOWING

"Megan Hartford's poetry is an invitation to explore life intimately, inciting us to notice the inherent worth and beauty in everything. *Worth Knowing* is worth reading—and out loud. As I read, I felt my body animate and my breath deepen. I felt more connected to everything. Megan writes, "The echo needs a voice." It is her voice that we need—honest and direct, precise yet lyrical. Her poems dig for secrets and explore the sensual; they are provocative love songs to humanity and to the Earth, investigating the dark and light equally. Each poem is a meditation on what is wild within us waiting on permission. Even after I finished reading this collection, I returned eagerly to reabsorb favorite lines with a fulfilling sigh. Her poetry will shapeshift your world and will—literally and figuratively—bring you back to life. I am grateful for Megan Hartford's voice. May *Worth Knowing* echo around the world." -Astara Raven, author of *How the Stars Tell Time*

"Within this collection of poems, Megan has managed to weave together a clever and lyrical depiction of just what the prairies and hills of the Midwest actually feel like, and what it means to be a part of this often misunderstood landscape, and the inhabitants that are lucky enough to be a part of it, and it a part of them. Poems that are so authentic to these surroundings, they are effortlessly devoured, one after another, like notes with a familiar resonation to them. From various perspectives, these poems are for everyone. So achingly beautiful, I want to steal them and turn them into songs." -Nathan Page, singer/songwriter

"Modest and melodic, this lovely collection pours words generously as warm tea from a pot for us to gently sip, steeped in curiosity, perseverance and wonder." -Meg Heriford, author of *Ladybird, Collected*

"In her book, *Worth Knowing*, Megan Hartford offers us a perspective on how to live in today's world. Her love of green growing things, her command to us to "Refuse!" to accept the past ways of living and her insistence for us not to despair. For as she says, our world contains those who are "laboriously looking into the darkness to share the light." And with her words, she invites us to do the same. *Worth Knowing* is her call to us...both women and men, both young and old, to change into new ways of being, of loving and of living life with the grace and elegance that is found within her poems." -Mary Elizabeth Atwood, painter, poet, thespian

"Megan's collection of poems, *Worth Knowing*, transfers sensation like an open, screen-free window to the wide, natural world. Each piece leads to internalization of this wonder and reminds readers that they are a part of it, not separate." -Sarah Romano Diehl, comic artist

Old Couch Press
Manhattan, Kansas

Worth Knowing

Library of Congress Control Number: 2023903831

ISBN 979-8-218-16154-5
ISBN 979-8-218-16155-2 (ebook)

Cover illustration and design by Liv Lee
www.livlee.com.au

Author photo by Meghan Tuttle

First paperback edition, 2023

To Beatrice and Willa,
the two people most worth knowing.

AUTHOR'S NOTE

This collection is composed entirely of found poems.

Found poems are created by piecing together words and/
or phrases from writings that already exist, anything from
other poems or books to articles, speeches or letters.

As an avid, long-time thrifter, the scavenging nature of
found poetry feels like home, akin to combing through
crowded racks of used clothing to find hidden gems into
which I can breathe new life.

For this collection of poems, I pulled from four informa-
tional texts from the Little Nature Library's 1917 Worth
Knowing series: *Trees Worth Knowing* by Julia Ellen Rogers,
Birds Worth Knowing by Neltje Blanchan, *Wildflowers Worth
Knowing* also by Neltje Blanchan, and *Butterflies Worth
Knowing* by Clarence M. Weed, all of which are in the public
domain. Each section of this book, *Existence, Expressions,
Earth,* and *Embodied,* contains poems created using one of
the four texts, respectively.

Working within the source material, I began, naturally, at
the beginning of each book, scanning through more than
1,000 total pages to find words and phrases that stood out
to me intuitively, underlining them and then piecing them

together until a poem began to emerge. I continued moving through the pages of the book, gathering bits and pieces, adding and subtracting here and there, until the poem felt complete. Some poems developed in only a few pages, while others took more than twenty pages to finish. An example of this process can be found on the opposite page.

In allowing poems to come forth in such a way, one parameter I gave myself was to keep the words in the order in which they appeared in the source material. For me, having these rigid boundaries actually allows me to be more creative. In this way, I'm able to cut a path through the material that leads me to my own poems.

I am reminded of this quote by Michelangelo: "Every block of stone has a statue inside it and it is the task of the sculptor to discover it." When I held each of these four books, working my way through them page by page, that is exactly how I felt: my poems were between the two covers, just waiting to be discovered.

-Megan Hartford

Found poetry process example
Source material: *Trees Worth Knowing*
by Julia Ellen Rogers

strength and beauty of tree architecture which the foliage conceals in summertime. The close-knit, alive-looking bark of a living tree they do not distinguish from the dull, loose-hung garment worn by the dead tree in the row. All trees look alike to them in winter.

Yet there is so much to see if only one will take time to look. Even the most heedless are struck at times with the mystery of the winter trance of the trees. They know that each spring reënacts the vernal miracle. Thoughtful people have put questions to these sphinx-like trees. Secrets the bark and bud scales hide have been revealed to those who have patiently and importunately inquired. A keen pair of eyes used upon a single elm in the dooryard for a whole year will surprise and inform the observer. It will be indeed the year of miracle.

A tree has no centre of life, no vital organs corresponding to those of animals. It is made up, from twig to root, of annual, concentric layers of wood around a central pith.

It is completely covered with a close garment of bark, also made of annual layers. Between bark and wood is the delicate undergarment of living tissue called *cambium*. This is disappointing when one comes to look for it, for all there is of it is a colorless, slimy substance that moistens the youngest layers of wood and bark, and forms the layer of separation between them. This cambium is the life of the tree. A hollow trunk seems scarcely a disability. The loss of limbs a tree can survive and start afresh. But girdle its trunk, exposing a ring of the cambium to the air, and the tree dies. The vital connection of leaves and roots is destroyed by the girdling; nothing can save the tree's life. Girdle a limb or a twig and all above the injury suffers practical amputation.

Resulting poem, *When The Veil Is Thin*,
found on page 59.

CONTENTS

EXISTENCE

A BLESSING FOR EXISTING

May we resist wind storms
and a transformed climate
to make the best of this journey.

LIFE IS

Life is

dashes of color,
giving more,
a struggle,
a delight,
being whole and curious and wild,
the sweetness in an exhale.

It is important and thorny and hard

and well worth it.

THE COLOR OF WATER

Life comes in,
the color of water.

It is found in the wounds.

Very often
it is in the interlacing fibers
of the wings.

It has a strict habit
of exceptional instances.

This tenacious life will exist
in each golden being.

It will enable us to belong.

IN EACH OF US

Untidy as it is,
life is streaked
with wonderful colors

that blend
to make
a gold whorl of glory

within.

TO ENDURE

Opening inside

stripped of
the notion,
the belief,
this idea,

that the life before you
should rise and flow
unimpeded.

It is worth knowing
that one cannot yield
to its hardness.

One heads forward
to conquer the unconquerable.

SUCH GREAT HEIGHTS

The mind awakening
to shed the old
for the interesting,

harmonizing
with the altitudes
of life.

THIS GOLDEN SPACE

Be in the moment
blending with the quiet beauty
of this golden space.

FORMS CARRIED FREELY

Forms carried freely,
reflecting the indomitable spirit
of living in the moment.

A PASSION FOR LIFE

Embers of lives on fire—
each wild, indomitable and spreading.

AN EAGERLY DEVOURED LIFE

At home in
the wilds of the heart,
the festival of patience,
the season of joy,
the carnival of growth.

Old-fashioned
and charmingly unconventional

with grace like music,
and roots beneath the soil,

head rising,
feet running up river banks
and over the prairies.

Indeed, an eagerly devoured life.

AN UNFOLDING

The root of the work
is in breathing

to open
to unfold

and be found.

IN A DAY

In a day

rise,
ground,
open,
and leave room
to grow.

LIKE THE WATER

The river submits readily
to the banks,
weaving with wonderful
lightness and grace
to the sea.

One has but to match
its grace,
and slowly but surely,
like the water,
they find they are free.

GOLD DUST

The scales of fulfillment
sway in the wind,
pushed around in a whorl,
becoming loose and pendulous
as the wind shakes them.

Soon
gold dust fills them.

They
hang
down
with the added weight.

The scales break

with the height and girth
of the magic of life

with the golden worth
of the soul.

PURSUING JOY

Loosen,
expand,
fade,

forming expanses,
passing through
changing hues.

The wayward arrangement of time.

A community of superlatives
where the breath
tempers the height.

More magnificent
than the spectacle
of surprises in spring.

It is wild.

It spreads in a whorl,
spreading
until
it is immortalized
in song and story.

MOVING BEYOND (WHAT THEY TOLD US TO BE)

desirable
handsome
sweet
slender
brilliant
rich

Each a planted parasite
that finds its food
within our own picture.

TO HEAL

The wound of perfection is as wide and
deep
as
the
sea.

Be soft.

Instead choosing grace.

LIFE: A STORY

Head lifted,
heart soft,
as life is precarious—

it grows,
is stunted,
becomes more rigorous,
becomes beautiful,
is marred,
defiled.

Its range is continuous.

And the heart can scarcely
make up for
the imperfect results
as love
stands alone
and holds its own.

There is no time in life
when it is not
a beautiful addition.

LOVE,

it grows like wheat in a field
when adorned with an abundance
of dancing sunlight.

WHEN WE BREATHE

And sometimes,
the exhales of the world
lengthen,
and its heart is wild
and it seems to feel at home.

TAKE CARE, DEAR ONE

In the heart
is a garden
that grows,

and in the depths of it
the fruit is ripe,
however no fruit is more delicate.

THE PECULIARITY OF THE HEART

The peculiarity of the heart—

It grows to its largest size
before
falling.

ON LOVE

A person says,
"I know love,

its power to confuse
and overwhelm,

its easily remembered traits,
familiar and dependable,

the rejoicing and singing."

A universal language—

its vocabulary,
its forms and usages
remain unchanged.

Though using them may be unreliable.

Many describe it
in books and music,
weeping,
and the heart flowers
and nobody hesitates.

A REASON FOR BEING

As a being bound
to the universal union
of pleasure
and the body,
one realizes
a surrender to
the story,

whose chapters
are full of heat
and colors ripening
in the season of warm days,

is the beauty of living.

WHEN IT'S GOOD, IT'S GOOD

A lover unfolding,
beginning to loosen,
to burn.

Fragrant flesh,
beautiful and heavy,
pungent and smooth.

A lover moist and wild,
skin soft
with the taste of soap.

An indelible stimulant
for being thoroughly alive.

LIKE HONEY

Like honey,
sweet and smooth.

Like soil,
moist and swelling.

A lover,
soft and ready.

Sprawling limbs
interlacing,
vine-like curves.

Worn out.
Must stop to rest.

Lovers ruddy
with delight.

THE PROMISE

Nothing is more beautiful
than the promise
of a new relationship.

Blossoming,
it grows
to
the
height
of a slender-branched tree.

Not a moment
lacks interest
for weeks.

Then,
comes the slow
fading.

Gradually,
the fade leaves the two
almost strangers,
and leaves a bitter taste
in both of them.

An experience
that will not be forgotten soon.

AND THE WIND IS WILD

When night comes, or
when rain begins to fall, and
that old chatter makes the years
become distorted and dark,
and the wind is wild,
choose a free and bare and imperfect heart
unmarred by change.

UNTIL THE WILD LEARNS

Wild years,
growing within
until the wild learns
that it is whole.

When one finds healing,
the transformation
is nothing short of a miracle.

A glow never quite lost.

NO GOLDEN SEASON

The wind shaped the world
into curious forms
and scatters us
into the landscape.

There is beauty
in the history
of the human race
and
those who
light the fire
that burns that beauty,
their heart used for fuel.

"In the old days"
was no golden season
for all.

BROUGHT BY THE WIND

Some hardship—

lined with gold-dust,
and brought by the wind—

is inevitably suffered.

One is strengthened
as they stand—
living,
bleeding,
growing,
weeping.

Open to life.

THE LIGHT

One contains the light within
and opens along the scar,
opens,
and sheds the dark beauty
of the winter,
shining the light—

of the heart,
of exceptional beauty,
of the lover, and
of wishes flowering
like buds in the spring.

ANOTHER WAY TO BE

We live crowded and compared.

Strength,
durability,
work,
preeminence
are highly valued.

It is possible to live
in resistance.

To be alive.

To cast off the veil
and persist.

TO THOSE WHO LIVE TO DISCOVER

To each who has patiently toiled,
willing to grow,
to withstand the straight line,
who live to discover.

At once spreading the light
and a lover of the dark.

Each drinking up
that which the wind
carries away.

Lives rich in myths and superstitions,
in wisdom and knowledge.

People curious and beautiful and bold.

TO OURSELVES

We belong only
to that which is within.

LIGHT THAT RISES

All people carry light
that rises from them,
nourishing the world.

AS THEY PLAY

They filled their pockets
with music for us,
making lives full
and loving
and sometimes tinted
with the soft light
of winter days or
the shade cast
by a tree in midsummer.

We look from our windows
as they play it,
and we smile.

WITH CURIOSITY

They wove their hopes
through life
crowned with curiosity.

GOLDEN

Bare, fleshy, natural,
a charming witch
with petals like gold threads,
veiled with gold flowers,
ethereal as the exhale
that comes
when the lips part.

She is a dream
in vivid colors,
a burning bush,
the soft sunshine
rested upon the flower.

EVER-BLOOMING

One grows older,
silver and golden,
glimpses of life
and its beauty
unfold,
and are carried
within,
ever-blooming.

AGE BEGETS BEAUTY

The hues of death
bear resemblance
to the hunt to retain youth.

As age advances
the bloom and color
of beauty
expands
and reaches
its greatest abundance.

ITS TENDER STRUCTURE

Life unfolding,
wrapped in the
miracle of beauty
more delicate than
the wind and the sun.

Its tender structure
a framework of wood
burning into ashes
at sunset
on a sunless day.

THE BEAUTY OF THE BARE HEART

A loss may be made good
in time.

It needs room
to be broken,
to grow tender.

The beauty of the bare heart
cracking open,
eager to be free.

WHEN THE VEIL IS THIN

The dead have secrets
revealed to those
who have patiently inquired.

Life,

the layer of separation
between them,

seems a vital connection.

A SPIRAL OF THREADS AND FIBERS

Time is woven
into a spiral

with threads
strong, dense, durable,

with fibers whose reach
has no end.

TO LIBERATE THE YEARS

Time is valuable,
is preeminent in importance,
and scattered with
hope, growth, beauty.

It is in dwindling supply
and strong demand.

Living wasteful of life and time,
lost in the years,
is a starved existence,
and the death of vitality.

To liberate the years,
seize each hour.

BREATH IS THE BRIDGE

Quiet breathing.

Incessantly.

Actively.

Breathing must go on,
day and night,
as long as life lasts.

Breathing.
Growing.
Alive.

BECOME

Continual inhales
and exhales,
finally passing into oblivion.

Empty, colorless living.

No substance,
no added breadth,
no growth.

Only alive in form.

Life comes only once.

Become a part of the story.

EXPRESSIONS

A POETRY OF MOTION

Bodies swallowed
by fear.

Bodies motionless and
wounded.

Bodies stuck
floating on the water.

But—

the water carries
a love song to
these bodies,

that are all at once
a poetry of motion,

rocked in the cradle
of the deep,

across reflected skies,

bodies able to rise.

LOVE IS BLUE

There is plenty of time
to cling to old-fashioned ways
and become dependent upon them.

Refuse.

Live in search of color—
a rich blue, with verdigris tints,
a deep blue, margined with light,
a slight tinge of blue, glowing indigo,
the blue sky singing.

Gaily dressed
with a glint of blue metallic
to attract the eye,

with no attempt at concealment,
sing the song of truth.

GATHERING IN THE DARK

Become still,

wait for a voice
strong and clear.

It rises above
the great variety
of sounds
to reveal a warning—

Only trust the light
gathering in the dark.

WALKING WITH A LANTERN

It has been suggested that
change can manifest a revival.

Certainty—too destructive
for survival.

Every measure ought to be taken
to preserve a voice
crying to awaken,

to foster the *humanity*
living among the convicted and condemned,
that is not afraid to live among them.

Ignorance,
a very dangerous thing—
destroyer
of land, of liberty,
found among many kinds.

But others emerge,
laboriously looking
in the darkness
to share the light.

WILD SENSE OF WONDER

Ignorant people's minds
are firmly fixed.

Therefore,
study, read, work,
intoxicated with
a wild sense of wonder,

and with a voice
that ripples
from human to human,
strong enough to
turn the head
to see
in different directions.

The echo needs a voice.

THERE IS NO OTHER

Persecutions of endless variety—

human rights molested,

the body
concealed,
shrouded,
and then devoured—
its flesh the prize.

Unmerciful persecution—

time heavily strewn with bones,

an accumulation of wings.

Every voice calls out
for life, liberty
and bodies safe
in a world with a searchlight
keeping in check the ceaseless
war against the "other".

OUR BETTER ANGELS

They destroy the unjust,
rising every day
with that in mind.

Living
to tip the scales
of justice.

Exposed.
Protecting.
Often buried.

Without so much as a "thank you."

We must not forget.

WELCOMED WORDS

Some have a reputation
for hearts in pain.

To them, the truth
is invaluable.

They are ever curious,
discovering that
pain concealed, poisons,
and that to destroy it,
with welcomed words,
can be the very poetry
of existence.

FOR EACH OF US

Express if freely.

Realizing.
Being.
Resting.

Worthy.

The day is dawning
for us all.

A SONG AT SUNRISE

The buzz of dawn grows.

It starts the morning chorus
after long periods of silence.

It punctuates everything
that might feel larger
than yourself.

Your breath,
a familiar refrain,
endures.

Notice it—

a song
swaying airily
along.

SHADOW WORK

Daylight sings in colors—
a touch of
scarlet,
olive,
yellow,
orange.

The night
swallows
the light
and sings
of the grace
gathering
in the dark.

SKY ABOVE, EARTH BELOW

Just after sunset
is a resting place.

The body stretches to open.

The sky and the earth
wait for life to still.

They hang themselves up
to go to sleep.

The boundless sky,
the most exquisite earth,

rest,

clinging to a love song
hidden
so
deep
that only the body
can find it.

BEYOND LIVING

A song bewitches,
carrying the heart
on the melody,

fluttering
and
restless,
fragile
and
fearless,

absorbed in
this song
that lives
beyond living.

Listen to it
over and over
again.

It is not often
that one can
get close enough
to recognize it

hidden there

within.

SING ITS NAME

You may be dreaming of it.

Constantly, restlessly
hunting for it.

Determined to
learn from it,
be warmed into life by it,
get lost in it.

With a gentle heart,
sing its name.

It calls out to you from within.

SIREN SONG

Her song dares you
to sing,
to open,
to discover
that you have
the sweetest of songs,

that the music within you
is magic.

WHEN IT SINGS

Dear,
dearie,
dearest,

the entire body,

like wildflowers
out in the sun,

blossoms
when it sings
to the earth,
living freely
on fire.

A LAUGH IS

A laugh
is the sound
of the life
you hope for.

A SIGNIFICANT EXPRESSION

I gather the wild wind—

a familiar companion.

Its soft whistling
sweeps by.

I dance,

meditating
on the swaying body
as a significant expression
of the wild.

A SONG FROM THE TREES

Here I am,
a song from the trees.

A heavenly song,
gracious and
full of confidence.

The opening notes
reflecting the wildness
no words can possibly convey.

Music
mysterious,
elusive,
melodious—

an ethereal hymn
fluttering among the leaves.

IF EVER YOU HAVE A CHANCE

Love.
Love.
Love.

The oft-repeated notes
echo above,
sometimes close enough
to touch,
sung softly
over and over again.

Notes uttered
sometimes in one key,
sometimes in another.

If ever you have a chance,
sit down quietly for a while
and wait for the song—
a melody to live in.

SOME SAY

Some say
it is a simple matter
of helping one another see
the flash of beauty
in the commonest of conditions.

TO BE HEARD

There is no lovelier sound
than the mouthfuls of silence
as you listen.

TO SING LOVE

Listen.

A tender lover
with a soft voice.

A lover to sing love.

Words on rounded wings
in flight
like
birds
of
a
feather.

Notes
streaked with
the cool of the morning,
the heat of noon,
the hush of evening.

Listen.

TO DANCE

Emerging with a movement
of impassioned grace,

the very poetry of motion
the very prose of existence

in pursuit of pleasure
through the body.

BODIES SING OF LOVE

Bodies sing of love.

Tender, naked bodies

humming,

wild like mighty rivers,

devoted,

loving,

lying close,

pressed against the breast,
and below,
legs feathered.

Their tender flesh
a love song.

Their musky flesh
in perfect harmony.

All their trust
is in the other.

THE WILD

Almost settled down,

then—

on fluttering wings
the wild
makes a nest
of her own
in the heart
and remains,
in light and dark.

All day long
you feed on the wild,

until a great transformation
has gradually taken place.

A change that nothing escapes.

And after—
blinking,
bewildered,

you cry,
laugh,
and fly away.

EARTH

AT DAWN

The promise of the day
opens with the dawn
and weaves a web
around the one who
is ready to take
its lesson to heart.

IN THE GOLDEN MORNING

In the golden morning
the earth is paradise,
with beauty,
regarded as sacred,
spreading
throughout the garden,
the meadows,
over the grass of dusty roadsides,
across continents,
sprawling,
clinging to the shadowy mountain stream,
soaking the open woods,
bursting,
wandering about the globe,
covering it in sunlight.

LIKE JEWELS

Beside streams,
like jewels from a lady's ear,
dewy morning leaves hung,
dancing,
sparkling in the sunshine.

A PAINTED LADY

This perfect earth,
with its knowing
and patience
and the movement
of its moon.

A painted lady
marked with a
delicate blue.

An exceedingly
hospitable,
abiding place.

Its secret
penetrating
all.

THE EARTH AND HER SOIL

Life quietly growing
in grassy places,
at home
in the meadows,
ditches,
and swamps—

devoted to
the earth
and
her soil.

AN ODE TO THE PRAIRIE

The grass is home
and filled with a certain magic.

A story told by its thread-like spires.

WHAT THE EARTH PROVIDES

When healers possess
a connection with
the herbage at our feet,
they delight in the
considerable importance of
the leaves,
flowers,
and roots
of plants.

Wanderers of
the prairie,
mountainsides,
woods and thickets,
they prepare
plasters,
ointments,
syrups,
and oils
to cure every ill.

Heir to their ancestors'
relics of study,

*(the shaded and sheltered,
the wild—*

*in the earth
or in a sunny window—*

spreading in the inaccessible crevice
or some wind-swept place
by the roadside),

they are one with Nature—
touched by it all.

Earth—
an apothecary for all.

AS SPRING APPROACHES

Vivid blue skies,

the earth
bright and buzzing,

brimming
with the dream
of clovers and bees.

FIRST THE FORSYTHIA

In this season
a lady's fragrant perfume
rises from the earth.

WARMING INTO LIFE

The fragrance of the very breath
of spring—
of soil
just warming into life.

No remnants of snowdrifts,
no reminders of winter.

The surprise at finding
dainty spring flowers
as warmer suns bring life
through dead leaves.

IN BLOOM

Life budding—
in connection
with
the soil below.

A symphony of pink,
like the flushed faces
of sweet lovers.

JUST BELOW

Tangled roots within the garden,
hidden just below
the conspicuous flowers,
generously giving
what is in the soil.

AND THE SUN

Under bright skies
the prairie blooms
with cheerful readiness
and the meadows
are radiant
with their blushing loveliness
and the sun,
that yellow eye in the sky,
can see it all.

ACROSS THE OPEN PRAIRIE

Meadows of soft, feathery grass
bearing the breeze
wrapped in sunshine,
with charm enough
to hold the dullest eye
and leave a lover blushing.

LIKE A POET

A wind blows
in a whorl,
bringing the hillsides
to life.

The movement
of these gales
is like a poet's
high-flown rhapsody—
beautiful and wild.

CHARMING THE EARTH

Occasionally,
the world sends forth
vivid music,

opening bodies
surreptitiously,
naturally,

with feet
barefoot
and graceful,
and curious,

charming the earth
with movements
of joyousness.

A REFUGE

Wading into shallow water
we observe the movement
of heavenly bodies,
conscious of the inner meaning
of the ponds and streams.

The water beneath leafy cathedral arches
is a refuge from what might have been.

A BAPTISM

The body healing
in the water of slow streams
must be remembered.

FLOATING FREE OF TIME

A hummingbird—
the messenger of Nature—
flying high and low,
most at home
among the phantastical spirits,
the witches,
and the superstitious.

LUNA

Moths,
like the moon,
blossom
in the deepening darkness.

They flutter above,
opened to the night,
wild and solitary.

AN ANCESTRAL LANDSCAPE

Naked fields
desire to be
uncultivated,
wild,
an ancestral landscape
laden with heavenly
purity, eternalized
in a whorl of color.

BREAKING GROUND

A practical perfecting
for the benefit of man,
greedily corrupted.

The beauty of the blossom and blades,
concealed in their cultivated fields.

The earth in a struggle
for freedom.

PILLAGING

Converging in a cornucopia
of hidden purposes.

(Doubtless,
working to drain
the beauty of the earth
for man's sole delight.)

So exquisitely hidden,
they manufacture
their own suffocation.

FOR LITTLE MORE THAN HONEY

The earth,
easily neglected—

the pungent odor
of waste lands and rubbish heaps,

degrading the life
of animal and vegetable,

the nefarious business
of modification,

the half-drowned coast
exhausted into a watery grave,

reversing the natural order of life.

We trespass upon
the birds, the ants, the honey bees,

and men slaughter
for little more than honey.

The horrors in this land of liberty,
suffocate the animals and poison the plants.

The forest deeply cut
in the name of propriety.

AN OFFERING

The earth,
with her grace
and bright beauty,
withering and drying up
from ocean to ocean,

poison in the air
and in the
shriveled stem
in sandy soil.

Defiant,
this lady
offers new life
to us
for free.

AN ACT OF RESISTANCE

Fields flowering,
solemnly protesting
the weeds, and
all notorious pilferers.

NO SMALL VIRTUE

I agree with Emerson—
a weed is a plant
whose virtues we
have not yet discovered.

But, it is no small virtue
to appear,
bloom,
adapt,
and spread
with zealous splendor.

THEY ARE SACRED

Weeds along the highway
and upon the edge of the lawn,
pleasing to the earth.

Spreading,
scattered,
banished by most.

However,
keen eyes
see they are sacred.

AN EXQUISITE TANGLE

The sun's rays scorched the fields,
dry fields,
old fields
that used to grow wild.

However, the prolific plants remain
on the shady roadsides
in an exquisite tangle.

Those who see beauty here
show a preference for
the wild state of nature.

PROPAGATION

Wild seeds in the sacred ground

arising from rambling roadsides,
curving along country lanes,
waking into life.

Dandelion—
the lady of the roadside.

BURSTING FORTH

Spared from the scythe,
preserving an unkempt,
untidy look,
which brightens the banks of streams
with whimsical forms bursting forth
everywhere,
put forth from seeds scattered in sandy soil.

A delightful eccentricity.

WHEN WE'RE GONE

Fencerows without farms,
weedy growth
along barbed-wire barriers,
clover fields
fade into nothing.

The earth seems given up
to a wild state.

The prairies let alone
to overrun the earth.

IN FAITH

The land,
every part of it
growing
in faith.

A SACRED SYMBOL

Autumn beauty
in the golden leaves
floating on still water —
a sacred symbol of the season.

IN A GOLDEN TWILIGHT

An autumn landscape of
golden thickets,
golden woodlands,
with leaves of gold
like sunshine.

And now,
the leaves are gone.

The autumn leaves
hanging
above the earth
are now one
with the soil.

Low down
where the yellow
turn brown,
and transform
into
the land,
they dream of
the winter above.

WAS ONCE

The glossy bronze carpet
beneath the snow
was once
the whorl of leaves
above the land.

WINTER IS

Winter is
snow-covered,
cold, and chaste,
yet filled with
Nature's grace
found
in the flame-colored shades
(apricot, salmon, orange, and vermillion)
of sunset skies,
in the white-edged
mountainsides,
in the overwhelming beauty
of the loneliest mountain road
lined with evergreen leaves.

Its beauty is not without honor
and freely tucked away
in the spring.

WINTER SOLSTICE

With the weight of exposing too much,
the sun slowly rises,
offers but a glimpse,
and is gone.

AT DUSK

Questions are carried away by the wind,
and set free
in the rocky hillsides,
along the borders of streams,
over mountains,
leaving behind the distant, fading
revelry of the day.

EMBODIED

OF THE EARTH

A body of the earth.

A life of value.

Beauty in blossom within
where it rests quietly
while its
roots
penetrate
deeply.

The earth found
a resting place—
a home within.

THE BODY IS A FIESTA

Being in motion
like a breath of wind—

life arising from
the surface of the skin,

life bending and spinning
in uncertainty.

Life emerges
having found shelter
in the body.

NOTICE THE BODY

The beauty of the body—
abdomen, organs, appendages, joints;
connecting, breathing, clasping;
transformations, change.

The stretching of soft skin.

Born free,
transformed into differing sizes —
remarkable.

Nature is wonderful,
unfolding in the exquisite beauty
of childhood, youth and age,
of opening and expanding bodies.

Notice the body.

COMING FORTH

The first signs
of movements
in the body.

The whole process
simultaneously
tender and bold,

steadily growing —

a sense of wonder.

A mother
and
her swollen
body.

The head pushes out.
The first sight of the face—
eyes and mouth.

The shock.

The coming forth of life.

A BODY BECOMING

Born a beautiful little creature
to a mother fatigued.

A body with deeper stories to be told.

A body becoming.

ABOUT THE BODY

The most interesting thing
about the body
is that
within it,
we become.

BODY BIBLIOTHÈQUE

The body—
its life-story
pierces,
absorbs,
changes.

Most search out the story of life
recorded upon the body,
but beneath the skin
is a lifetime of histories,
hiding,
ready to escape.

BENEATH THE SKIN

Beneath the skin
wings expand,
opening and closing
in beautiful iridescent purples
and a spangled effect
of silver-white and brown
arranged in a complicated pattern
like splendid flowers
in a dense thicket.

A butterfly resting
within the body,
surrounded by
its blossoms.

THE INTERNAL MADE EXTERNAL

The skin breaks open
revealing butterflies
fluttering
from place to place.

A spiritual expedition.

Life rests upon a wing.

ON THE BREEZE

The autumn air
wafted on the breeze,
flitting from tree to tree—
willow,
poplar,
elm,
birch,
hackberry,
and also upon
the leaves of rose bushes,
following the butterflies
along the borders of woods
or in open glades.

Butterflies
that were curious
about the delicate blossoms
of my body.

THIS BODY HELD

On the plains
the color is striking—
still, green grass from the hills
to the lowland meadows.

The plains
in contrasting colors,
dazzling, brilliant colors,
illuminating and concealing.

Colors that mimic the sun.

Little attention given to this body
held by the wind-swept grasses,
indistinguishable from its surroundings.

A SOFT TOUCH

A striking golden hue
painted across
the body in its natural state.

Satisfied,
the body remains quiet,
in touch with itself,
safe.

The sun brings forth
a story
to be told by the wind.

PHEROMONES

A fragrance.

The hunt for sexual attraction.
Scents attractive to the senses.
Aromatic scents magnified and highly desirable.

A fragrance emitted.

Regardless of obstacles,
of long distances,
one will seek
a silken body to hold,
fragile crevices, openings,
known extensively,
to exhaustion.

They may lie motionless
for a considerable period,
resting.

However, places in the body
show signs of life.
No clothing concealing
those parts—
the body exposed.

The bodies,
these bodies,
flavored from
excessive stimulation,
bodies brilliantly curious,
constantly exploring.

The beauty lies
in the connection
and
in the pursuit.

AN EXPEDITION

The lovers disclose their forms.

Each clinging to the other,
coming together,
swaying back and forth.

The body discovered.

COALESCE

Eye to eye,
bodies curious,
suggestive.

These intergrading forms,

their movements grow slow,
prolonging the experience.

This escape overtakes them.

Eye to eye,
they seek out
shrouded limbs.

They partake of each other
in desirable, ever-present wonder.

LIKE LOVERS

The face,
the eyes,
the neck,
held by silken threads,
connected
with the body
and
with the knowledge of the body
like lovers.

ALL BODIES ARE GOOD BODIES

A glance
and
the eyes
notice
the marvelous beauty
that festoons
the body.

AS IT IS

A river is found
in the expanse of fields and meadows—
flowers are abundant,
no two exactly alike,
variation in form and color,
all remarkable.

And then, it happens—
we give one
a decided advantage
over the others
because of its
smaller leaves,
developed stem,
distinct color.

Any having characteristics
similar to it
are then likely
to become
some of the few flowers
to be seen as
essential,
notable,
favorable,

while others,
that are different
are rarely considered.

And then,
the butterflies
begin to appear
along with the summer.

They fly freely
in the fields and meadows
on expanded wings.

Of all the many kinds of flowers,
each is beautiful
to the butterflies.

Each one splendid as it is.

BEYOND THE BINARY

The flower blossoms.

They change the story
of their body.

Curious,
perhaps you ask...
perhaps you are wondering...
or assume...

Honey,
the only plausible explanation
is that
they are wonderful and beautiful
as they are.

IN THE BEAUTIFUL SILHOUETTE

Black-bodied
like black diamonds.

Bodies with silken skin.

Bodies in resistance
generation after generation.

Their existence,
their lives,
blossom in the most
remarkable manner.

Stems, leaves, flowers,
emerge
strong and abundant
in the beautiful silhouette
of the Black body.

LIKE A SILKEN WEB

Black skin
threads itself like
a silken web
about the body.

THE GARDEN OF THE BODY

Perhaps chosen bodies
are round and abundant
so that
the garden of the body
has the expanse
to flower and fruit.

FREE TO BE

Small, slender bodies,
angular in their structure.

The natural body,
changing.

Large bodies,
curving.

Stout bodies,
short and thick.

Considerable variation,
considerable life-histories.

The body,
free to be
as it is.

CURIOUS BODIES

A body that is mature,
with lines upon the face,
and a white streak
marking coppery-brown hair.

A wanderer,
frequenting flowery fields
where other wanderers congregate
by brooks and ponds.

However,
that wandering is
not aimless,
but rather,
curious bodies
that intermingle with life,
free, open.

A distinguished body
that is whole
and remarkable.

Bodies living well
to the end.

ACKNOWLEDGMENTS

Thank you to my creativity group: Ann Carter, Cindy Burr, Danielle Tarner, Gayle Doll, Kaisha Lawrence, Ginny Arthur, Molly Bernstein, Karen Hummel, and especially Deborah Murray without whom this collection would not exist. Deborah, thank you for your ever-present guidance, suggestions, encouragement and support.

To *Heron Tree*, thank you for being the first to publish my found poems, giving me the confidence to keep going.

To Andrea Glinn, thank you, dear friend, for pushing me to start writing again and for co-creating a space to give that writing a home, and for modeling what it looks like to live a bold and creative life, AND for being one of my closest friends and confidants for more than two decades.

To Suzanne Gatz, thank you for your feedback and leading the way as a fearless female.

To Nathan Page, thank you for spending so much time with each poem in this book. Your careful, conscientious commentary and confidence in my writing gave me the final push I needed to bring this book into this tangible form.

To my Coven sisters: Nancy Davis, Karen Seay, Heather McCornack, Kris Springer and Mary Elizabeth Atwood, thank you for the magic you have brought into my life and for seeing me and celebrating me, always.

To Shana Puckett and Oakley Shaw, thank you both for opening up new worlds within me, offering loving, unconditional guidance and holding a safe space for me to grow and expand.

To Lauren Page and Sarah Kinder, thank you for your friendship. Without you helping me clear a path, my life would have become too overgrown to bring this book into fruition.

To my family, thank you for giving me the space to follow my curiosity, and the confidence to continue picking myself back up.

To Ike, thank you for always being an attentive and admiring audience. Your support of my writing over the years is unparalleled. Your encouragement and enthusiasm have kept me writing and pushing myself beyond what I thought I was capable of.

To Beatrice and Willa, becoming your mother has been my greatest creative endeavor and has opened up a well of creativity within me that would never have been possible without each of you. Thank you for choosing me.

And finally, a deep, deep thank you to my Grammie, the late Mary Detwiler, who believed in me so wholeheartedly from the very beginning, as a 10-year-old writing poetry, that she submitted my very first poems to her local newspaper, *The Pratt Tribune*, who printed them, giving me my first publication.

SOURCE MATERIAL

Blanchan,Neltje. *Birds Worth Knowing*. Published by
 Doubleday, Doran and Company, Inc., 1917.
Blanchan, Neltje. *Wildflowers Worth Knowing*. Published by
 Doubleday and Company, Inc., 1917.
Rogers, Julia E. *Trees Worth Knowing*. Published by
 Doubleday, Page and Company, 1917.
Weed, Clarence M. *Butterflies Worth Knowing*. Published by
 Doubleday, Doran and Company, Inc., 1917.

ABOUT THE AUTHOR

Megan Hartford is a poet, activist, follower of curiosity, book reader, garden tender, seeker, student and teacher living with her two daughters in Manhattan, Kansas. @meganinthemorning